THE YEAR WITHOUT A SUMMER

How the 1815 Eruption of Mount Tambora Shaped History and Transformed the World

TIMELESS TALES

Table of contents

Introduction

The Year Without a Summer, 1816, stands as one of history's most remarkable and devastating natural events. Also known as the Poverty Year or Eighteen Hundred and Froze to Death, this year was marked by severe and anomalous weather patterns that led to widespread agricultural failures, famine, and socio-economic turmoil across the Northern Hemisphere. The root cause of this climate catastrophe was the eruption of Mount Tambora in Indonesia in April 1815, one of the most powerful volcanic eruptions in recorded history. The sheer scale and impact of this eruption sent ripples across the globe, dramatically altering the course of human history.

To understand the significance of the Year Without a Summer, it is essential to delve into the circumstances surrounding the Mount Tambora eruption and the subsequent climatic anomalies it triggered. Mount Tambora's eruption ejected an estimated 160 cubic kilometers of volcanic material into the atmosphere, releasing vast amounts of volcanic ash and sulfur dioxide. These particles formed a reflective aerosol layer in the stratosphere, which significantly reduced the amount of sunlight reaching the Earth's surface. This phenomenon, known as a volcanic winter, led to a substantial drop in global temperatures, creating unprecedented weather patterns and climatic disturbances.

The climatic consequences of the Year Without a Summer were felt far and wide, with the most severe impacts recorded in North America and Europe. Unseasonably cold temperatures, heavy rainfall, and persistent cloud cover dominated these regions, leading to a series of agricultural disasters. Frosts were reported as late as July and August in some areas, decimating crops and leading to food shortages. The agricultural crisis triggered a cascade of socio-economic challenges, including famine, disease outbreaks, and widespread social unrest.

The impact on agriculture was particularly devastating. In North America, the northeastern United States and parts of Canada experienced crop failures that resulted in skyrocketing food prices and widespread hunger. The lack of a reliable food supply forced many families to migrate westward in search of better opportunities. Similarly, Europe faced its own agricultural calamities, with heavy rains and cold temperatures destroying wheat, corn, and other staple crops. The resulting food shortages led to a sharp increase in food prices, exacerbating the plight of the poor and leading to food riots and social unrest in several countries.

The Year Without a Summer also had significant health implications. Malnutrition weakened populations, making them more susceptible to diseases such as typhus and cholera. The combination of famine and disease created a public health crisis that overwhelmed existing medical infrastructure and further strained social systems. The mortality rates during this period were alarmingly high, particularly among vulnerable populations such as children and the elderly.

The socio-economic effects of the Year Without a Summer extended beyond immediate food shortages and health crises. The economic downturn caused by the agricultural collapse led to widespread unemployment and financial instability. Many small farmers and laborers, unable to sustain their livelihoods, were forced into poverty. The social fabric of communities was tested as families and individuals struggled to survive in the face of adversity. Migration became a common response to the dire conditions, with many people leaving their homes in search of better prospects. In Europe, the mass movement of people contributed to social tensions and heightened political instability.

Culturally, the Year Without a Summer left an indelible mark on literature, art, and daily life. The gloomy, cold, and unpredictable weather inspired a sense of foreboding and despair that found expression in the works of contemporary writers and artists. Mary Shelley, for instance, wrote her seminal novel "Frankenstein" during the cold and dreary summer of 1816, while staying in Switzerland with Lord Byron and Percy Bysshe Shelley. The novel's themes of creation, destruction, and the consequences of human ambition can be seen as a reflection of the tumultuous times. Similarly, Lord Byron's poem "Darkness" echoes the pervasive sense of gloom and apocalyptic dread that characterized the period.

The Year Without a Summer also spurred scientific inquiry and advancements. The unusual weather patterns and their apparent link to the volcanic eruption of Mount Tambora prompted early meteorological studies and increased interest in understanding the Earth's climate system. These investigations laid the groundwork for the fields of volcanology and climatology, helping scientists to better comprehend the complex interactions between volcanic activity and climate. The lessons learned from 1816 have informed our understanding of subsequent volcanic events and their potential impacts on global climate.

The legacy of the Year Without a Summer is profound and far-reaching. The long-term climatic and environmental changes triggered by the volcanic eruption of Mount Tambora had lasting effects on ecosystems and agriculture. The economic and social upheavals experienced during this period left an indelible mark on the affected regions, influencing subsequent policies and societal developments. The historical significance of this event serves as a stark reminder of the vulnerability of human societies to natural disasters and the importance of resilience and adaptation in the face of environmental challenges.

In reflecting on the Year Without a Summer, it is crucial to acknowledge the resilience and adaptability of human societies. Despite the immense hardships and suffering, communities found ways to cope, adapt, and rebuild. The shared experience of adversity fostered a sense of solidarity and innovation, prompting new agricultural practices, social reforms, and scientific advancements. The lessons from 1816 resonate today, as we continue to grapple with the impacts of climate change and other environmental challenges.

In this book, we will explore the Year Without a Summer from multiple perspectives, providing a comprehensive account of its causes, effects, and legacy. We will delve into the geological and climatic events that precipitated this period of crisis, examine the socio-economic and cultural impacts on affected regions, and reflect on the scientific advancements and lessons learned. Through this exploration, we aim to illuminate the profound and far-reaching consequences of this extraordinary year and underscore the enduring relevance of its lessons for our contemporary world.

Chapter 1

Description

The Year Without a Summer stands as a stark example of nature's power to disrupt human life, marked by a severe agricultural crisis that historian John D. Post described as "the last great subsistence crisis in the Western world." The year 1816 brought unparalleled climatic anomalies that profoundly affected New England, Atlantic Canada, and Western Europe, leading to widespread food shortages and economic distress.

The primary catalyst for these anomalies was the catastrophic eruption of Mount Tambora in April 1815, located in Sumbawa, Indonesia. This eruption is noted for its extraordinary magnitude, earning a Volcanic Explosivity Index (VEI) of 7. It expelled at least 37 cubic kilometers (8.9 cubic miles) of dense-rock equivalent material into the atmosphere, making it the most recent confirmed VEI-7 eruption in history. The immense volume of volcanic ash and sulfur dioxide ejected into the stratosphere formed a global layer of sulfuric acid aerosols, which significantly reduced the amount of sunlight reaching the Earth's surface.

In addition to Tambora, several other substantial volcanic eruptions occurred in the early 19th century, contributing to the atmospheric dust load. These included the 1808 mystery eruption in the southwestern Pacific Ocean, the eruptions of La Soufrière in Saint Vincent and Awu in the Sangihe Islands in 1812, Suwanosejima in the Ryukyu Islands in 1813, and Mayon in the Philippines in 1814. Each of these eruptions, with a VEI of at least 4, added to the atmospheric particulate matter that further blocked sunlight, contributing to a significant drop in global temperatures.

A 2012 study by Berkeley Earth determined that the Tambora eruption alone caused a temporary decrease in the Earth's average land temperature by about one degree Celsius. Smaller, but still notable, temperature declines were also recorded as a result of the eruptions between 1812 and 1814. This period of cooling was exacerbated by the fact that the Earth was already experiencing the Little Ice Age, a centuries-long phase of cooler climate that had begun in the 14th century and caused significant agricultural challenges in Europe. The Tambora eruption, occurring near the end of the Little Ice Age, intensified the existing climatic cooling, compounding the hardship faced by many regions.

Adding to the climatic complexity, the Year Without a Summer coincided with the Dalton Minimum, a period of reduced solar activity from 1790 to 1830. May 1816 recorded an exceptionally low Wolf number, a measure of sunspot activity, at 0.1—the lowest since systematic observations of solar activity began. Although the precise impact of solar activity variations on Earth's climate remains uncertain, the correlation between the Dalton Minimum and the cooling of 1816 suggests a potential interplay that warrants further investigation.

The Year Without a Summer's impact on agriculture was catastrophic. The reduced temperatures and altered weather patterns led to widespread crop failures. In North America, the northeastern United States and parts of Canada experienced severe frosts as late as July and August, destroying vital crops and leading to food shortages. The resulting economic distress prompted mass migrations and exacerbated social tensions. In Europe, incessant rains and unseasonable cold devastated wheat, corn, and other staple crops, causing a dramatic increase in food prices and sparking food riots and unrest in several regions.

The agricultural failures and subsequent food scarcity led to widespread malnutrition and increased susceptibility to diseases such as typhus and cholera. The public health crisis overwhelmed the already strained medical infrastructure, leading to high mortality rates, particularly among vulnerable populations. The socio-economic consequences were profound, with widespread unemployment and financial instability pushing many into poverty.

Culturally, the Year Without a Summer influenced literature and the arts, reflecting the period's pervasive sense of gloom and foreboding. The bleak weather and dire circumstances inspired Mary Shelley to write "Frankenstein" during the cold, dismal summer of 1816 while staying in Switzerland with Lord Byron and Percy Bysshe Shelley. Lord Byron's poem "Darkness" captures the apocalyptic mood of the time, mirroring the societal despair caused by the relentless cold and darkness.

Scientific interest in the unusual weather patterns and their connection to the volcanic eruption of Mount Tambora spurred early meteorological studies and advances in understanding the Earth's climate system. These investigations laid the groundwork for the fields of volcanology and climatology, helping scientists to comprehend the complex interactions between volcanic activity and climate. The insights gained from studying the Year Without a Summer have informed our understanding of subsequent volcanic events and their potential global impacts.

Africa

While there is no direct evidence documenting conditions in the Sahel region during the Year Without a Summer, surrounding areas suggest that this region experienced above-normal rainfall. In contrast, the coastal regions of West Africa, located south of the Sahel, likely faced below-average precipitation levels. This period of climatic upheaval also impacted the Southern Hemisphere, notably affecting the South African coast with severe winter storms. A particularly violent storm struck near Cape Town on July 29-30, 1816, characterized by fierce northerly winds and hail. This storm caused significant damage to ships in the area, highlighting the extensive reach and varied impacts of the climatic anomalies during this extraordinary year.

The climatic disturbances of 1816 were part of a broader pattern of global weather anomalies caused by the massive eruption of Mount Tambora. The resulting volcanic ash and aerosols dispersed in the stratosphere, altering weather patterns worldwide. These shifts in atmospheric conditions brought unseasonable weather to various regions, impacting agriculture, economies, and daily life. In Africa, the differential impact on rainfall between the Sahel and the coastal regions underscores the complexity of these climate effects. The severe storm near Cape Town illustrates how even distant regions were not spared from the turmoil, experiencing extreme weather events that disrupted local life and commerce. This multifaceted impact of the Year Without a Summer offers a compelling example of how interconnected and vulnerable global climates can be to significant volcanic events.

Asia

The Year Without a Summer had far-reaching impacts on Asia, disrupting the monsoon season in China and causing severe floods in the Yangtze Valley. Fort Shuangcheng experienced fields damaged by frost and widespread desertion among conscripts. Unusual weather events, such as summer snowfall and mixed precipitation, were recorded in Jiangxi and Anhui. Taiwan saw snow in Hsinchu and Miaoli and frost in Changhua. These anomalies contributed to a large-scale famine in Yunnan, which significantly weakened the Qing dynasty's hold on power.

In India, the delayed summer monsoon led to late torrential rains, exacerbating a cholera outbreak that originated near the Ganges in Bengal and spread as far as Moscow. During the winter monsoon, Bengal experienced abnormal cold and snowfall, further stressing the region.

Japan, still wary from the Great Tenmei famine of 1782-1788, faced crop damage due to the cold. However, unlike other regions, Japan did not experience crop failures or significant population impacts, thanks in part to its cautious preparations.

The climatic disruptions of 1816, triggered by the eruption of Mount Tambora, highlighted the interconnectedness of global weather patterns and their profound impact on societies. China's disrupted monsoon season, India's cholera outbreak, and Taiwan's unexpected snowfall illustrate how volcanic activity can have wide-ranging and severe consequences. These events also underscore the resilience and adaptability required to cope with such unprecedented natural disasters. The Qing dynasty's decline in Yunnan and Japan's relative stability provide contrasting examples of how societies responded to the challenges posed by the Year Without a Summer.

Europe

The series of volcanic eruptions in the 1810s, culminating with Mount Tambora's massive eruption in 1815, set the stage for a period of severe agricultural decline. Europe, already struggling to recover from the Napoleonic Wars, faced devastating food shortages that led to its worst famine of the century. Persistent low temperatures and heavy rains caused widespread harvest failures in Great Britain and Ireland. Particularly in Ireland, the collapse of wheat, oat, and potato crops led to rampant famine in both the north and southwest regions, driving food prices to unprecedented heights across Europe.

The inability to pinpoint the exact cause of these climatic anomalies led to widespread panic and unrest. Desperate and hungry, people began to gather and protest outside grain markets and bakeries, culminating in violent food riots in many European cities. While such riots were not uncommon during times of scarcity, the disturbances of 1816 and 1817 were the most violent since the French Revolution. These riots underscored the severe social and economic strain caused by the catastrophic weather conditions.

The period between 1816 and 1819 also saw significant public health crises, notably major typhus epidemics that ravaged parts of Europe, including Ireland, Italy, Switzerland, and Scotland. The famine and subsequent malnutrition weakened populations, making them more susceptible to disease. In Ireland alone, the typhus epidemic claimed more than 65,000 lives as the disease spread across the continent.

Meteorological records, such as the long-running Central England temperature record, noted 1816 as the eleventh coldest year since 1659, with the third coldest summer and the coldest July ever recorded. These extreme weather conditions also caused widespread flooding of major rivers throughout Europe and unseasonable frost in August. In Hungary, snowfall was tinted brown by volcanic ash, while northern Italy experienced red snow throughout the year.

In western Switzerland, the cold summers of 1816 and 1817 led to the formation of an ice dam below the Giétro Glacier in the Val de Bagnes, creating a large lake. Despite the efforts of engineer Ignaz Venetz to mitigate the danger by draining the lake, the ice dam eventually collapsed in June 1818. The catastrophic flood that ensued claimed the lives of forty people, illustrating the deadly impact of the prolonged cold and unusual weather patterns.

North America

In the spring and summer of 1816, the eastern United States experienced a persistent "dry fog," which turned the sunlight red and dim enough to make sunspots visible to the naked eye. This fog, later identified by Clive Oppenheimer as a "stratospheric sulfate aerosol veil," neither dispersed with wind nor rain.

For those accustomed to long winters, the weather itself was not the primary hardship. Instead, the real challenge arose from its devastating impact on crops, which in turn affected the supply of food and firewood. Higher elevations, where farming was already difficult, were hit the hardest. In May 1816, frost destroyed most crops in the highlands of Massachusetts, New Hampshire, Vermont, and upstate New York. Snow fell in Albany, New York, and Dennysville, Maine, on June 6. In Cape May, New Jersey, frost was reported for five consecutive nights in late June, causing extensive crop damage. While some fruits and vegetables survived in New England, the corn ripened poorly, with only about a quarter being edible, and much of it was moldy and unfit even for animal feed.

The crop failures in New England, Canada, and parts of Europe caused food prices to spike. In Canada, Quebec ran out of bread and milk, forcing Nova Scotians to resort to boiling foraged herbs for sustenance. Sarah Snell Bryant from Cummington, Massachusetts, succinctly described the situation in her diary as "Weather backward." At the Church Family of Shakers near New Lebanon, New York, Nicholas Bennet wrote in May 1816 that "all was froze," and the hills appeared "barren like winter." In June, temperatures frequently fell below freezing, and the Shakers had to replant crops destroyed by the cold on June 12. By July 7, the cold was so severe that all crops had ceased growing. Edward Holyoke, a physician and amateur astronomer in Salem, Massachusetts, observed on June 7 in Franconia, New Hampshire, that the ground was frozen hard with snow squalls throughout the day, and icicles were 12 inches long even in the midday shade. The brief lull in cold weather ended abruptly in August, when temperatures again plummeted, destroying what little was left of the bean and corn crops.

Massachusetts historian William G. Atkins summarized the disaster, noting that severe frosts occurred every month, and June 7 and 8 saw snow so cold that it froze crops down to their roots. In early autumn, corn was so thoroughly frozen that it never ripened and was hardly worth harvesting. Bread was scarce, prices were high, and the poorer classes often faced severe food shortages. The lack of an extensive railroad network at the time meant that people had to rely on local resources, exacerbating the crisis.

In July and August, ice was observed on lakes and rivers as far south as northwestern Pennsylvania. Frost hit Virginia on August 20 and 21, and rapid, dramatic temperature swings were common, with temperatures occasionally dropping from 95°F (35°C) to near-freezing within hours. Thomas Jefferson, retired at Monticello, suffered crop failures that further deepened his debt. A Virginia newspaper reported on September 13 that corn crops would fall short by half to two-thirds, lamenting that "the cold as well as the drought has nipped the buds of hope." Another report from Norfolk, Virginia, described a chilly summer, with easterly winds prevailing for nearly three months, overcast skies, and damp, uncomfortable air making the fireside a desirable retreat.

Despite some regional farmers managing to bring crops to maturity, the price of grains soared. For instance, the price of oats skyrocketed from 12¢ per bushel in 1815 to 92¢ per bushel in 1816. The crop failures were further aggravated by inadequate transportation infrastructure, as the absence of roads, navigable inland waterways, and railroads made importing food prohibitively expensive in most parts of the country.

Maryland experienced brown, bluish, and yellow snowfall in April and May, colored by volcanic ash in the atmosphere, highlighting the extensive reach and impact of the volcanic activity from the eruption of Mount Tambora. These atmospheric anomalies underscore the global extent of the climatic disruptions during the Year Without a Summer and the profound challenges they posed to human societies.

South America

An account from northeastern Brazil, published in the United Kingdom, detailed the severe drought that plagued the region in early 1817. Reports from Pernambuco on February 8th revealed that an extraordinary drought had affected the tropical areas between Pernambuco and Rio de Janeiro. This prolonged dry spell dried up all the streams, causing widespread devastation among cattle, which were either dying or already dead. The local population, desperate for water, migrated en masse to the borders of the major rivers.

The drought's impact was severe, leading to significant distress due to the lack of provisions. The mills, essential for processing food, were completely inoperative. The absence of windmills in the region compounded the problem, as there was no way to grind corn into flour. To address this dire situation, vessels were dispatched from Pernambuco to the United States to procure flour.

Complicating matters further was the disruption of the coastal trade, driven by fears of war with Buenos Aires. This interruption exacerbated the already critical food shortages, as it hindered the flow of essential supplies. The local economy was brought to a standstill, with mills inactive and agricultural production severely hampered.

The drought in northeastern Brazil illustrates the far-reaching effects of climatic anomalies during this period. It underscores how regions reliant on specific weather patterns for agriculture and water supply were particularly vulnerable. The desperation of the population, forced to relocate in search of water, highlights the severe human impact of environmental changes. This situation also underscores the interconnectedness of global trade, as the drought prompted international efforts to secure essential supplies, illustrating how local climatic events can have global repercussions.

Chapter 2

The Eruption of April 1815

The eruption of Mount Tambora in April 1815 stands as one of the most significant and cataclysmic volcanic events in recorded history. This colossal eruption not only had immediate and devastating effects on the local environment and populations but also induced global climatic changes that led to the infamous "Year Without a Summer" in 1816.

Mount Tambora, located on the island of Sumbawa in Indonesia, had been dormant for centuries before its dramatic reawakening in 1815. The eruption began on April 5, with small to moderate explosions that continued for several days. However, these initial outbursts were mere preludes to the main event. On April 10, the volcano unleashed a paroxysmal eruption that would alter the course of global history.

The April 10 eruption was of an unprecedented scale, rated as a 7 on the Volcanic Explosivity Index (VEI), making it the most powerful volcanic event of the 19th century. The eruption column reached a staggering height of over 40 kilometers (25 miles) into the stratosphere. The sheer volume of material ejected was astounding: at least 37 cubic kilometers (8.9 cubic miles) of dense-rock equivalent tephra were blasted into the atmosphere. This immense amount of ash and volcanic gasses, primarily sulfur dioxide, spread around the globe, causing significant climatic disruptions.

The immediate local effects of the eruption were catastrophic. The explosion was heard as far away as Sumatra, over 2,000 kilometers (1,240 miles) away. Pyroclastic flows—fast-moving currents of hot gas and volcanic matter—swept down the slopes of Tambora, obliterating everything in their path. The surrounding region was buried under a thick layer of ash, causing the collapse of houses and buildings. The island of Sumbawa was virtually unrecognizable, with an estimated 10,000 to 12,000 people killed directly by the eruption and its immediate aftermath.

The wider impact on the Indonesian archipelago was also devastating. The massive release of volcanic ash and aerosols into the atmosphere led to darkness across the region for several days. Crops were destroyed, and water sources were contaminated, leading to widespread famine and disease. It is estimated that an additional 70,000 to 90,000 people died in the subsequent months due to starvation and illnesses exacerbated by the eruption.

The far-reaching effects of the eruption were not confined to Indonesia. The vast quantities of sulfur dioxide released into the stratosphere formed sulfate aerosols, which spread around the globe and significantly reduced the amount of sunlight reaching the Earth's surface. This led to a dramatic and abrupt change in global climate patterns. The year 1816 came to be known as the "Year Without a Summer," as the volcanic winter triggered by the eruption caused temperatures to drop worldwide.

In Europe and North America, the summer of 1816 was marked by unusually cold and wet conditions. Frosts and snowfalls were reported in June and July, and the growing season was severely shortened. Crops failed across the Northern Hemisphere, leading to food shortages and sharp increases in food prices. The resultant famine and social unrest had profound effects on societies. In Europe, still recovering from the Napoleonic Wars, the agricultural collapse contributed to widespread poverty and instability. In North America, communities struggled to cope with the harsh conditions, with many families forced to abandon their farms and move westward in search of better prospects.

The climatic disruptions also had significant cultural and scientific impacts. The bleak and dreary conditions of the "Year Without a Summer" are said to have inspired literary works such as Mary Shelley's "Frankenstein" and Lord Byron's poem "Darkness." Additionally, the strange and dramatic weather events spurred scientific interest in studying the connections between volcanic activity and climate change, laying the groundwork for the emerging field of volcanology and climatology.

The eruption of Mount Tambora is a stark reminder of the power of natural forces and their ability to reshape human history. It also underscores the interconnectedness of global systems, as a single volcanic event in Indonesia could have such profound and widespread effects on climate, agriculture, and society around the world.

In the years following the eruption, the study of volcanic eruptions and their impacts has become a crucial area of scientific inquiry. The data gathered from the Tambora eruption has provided valuable insights into the mechanisms of volcanic activity and its effects on the atmosphere. Scientists now recognize the importance of monitoring volcanic activity and understanding the potential for similar events to occur in the future.

Modern technology and advances in volcanology have significantly improved our ability to predict and respond to volcanic eruptions. Early warning systems, satellite monitoring, and better understanding of volcanic processes have increased our preparedness for future events. However, the Tambora eruption serves as a humbling reminder of the limitations of human control over natural phenomena.

In addition to its scientific legacy, the Tambora eruption has also left a lasting impact on the cultural and historical landscape. The stories and records from 1815 and 1816 offer poignant reminders of human resilience in the face of natural disasters. Communities around the world struggled to adapt to the extreme conditions, and their experiences have been preserved in diaries, letters, and historical accounts.

Furthermore, the Tambora eruption has highlighted the need for global cooperation in addressing the challenges posed by natural disasters. The international response to the "Year Without a Summer" was limited by the communication and transportation technologies of the time. Today, the global community is better equipped to share information, resources, and expertise in the face of such crises, emphasizing the importance of collaboration and solidarity.

Chapter 3

Societal effects

High levels of tephra in the atmosphere following the eruption created a pervasive haze that lingered for several years, imparting rich red hues to sunsets. Artistic works from the years surrounding the event reflect this change, portraying more somber and darker scenes even in daylight. For example, Caspar David Friedrich's paintings such as "The Monk by the Sea" (ca. 1808–1810) and "Two Men by the Sea" (1817) illustrate this shift in mood.

A study conducted in 2007 analyzed paintings from 1500 to 1900, correlating notable volcanic events with an increased use of red in artwork. The tephra in the atmosphere not only led to vivid sunsets, as depicted in J. M. W. Turner's works like "Chichester Canal" (1828), but also influenced the predominant yellow tones in his paintings. Similar atmospheric effects were observed after the 1883 eruption of Krakatoa and the 1991 eruption of Mount Pinatubo, impacting the West Coast of the United States.

The shortage of oats to feed horses following the eruption may have spurred the German inventor Karl Drais to seek alternatives to horseless transportation, leading to the creation of the draisine and velocipede, early forms of the bicycle.

The agricultural failures during the "Year without a Summer" prompted significant migration within the United States. Thousands left New England for western New York and the Northwest Territory, seeking better climates and soil conditions for farming. This migration played a role in shaping the Midwest; Indiana became a state in December 1816, followed by Illinois two years later. Historian Lawrence Goldman suggests that the influx of settlers into upstate New York's burned-over district contributed to the prominence of the abolitionist movement there.

Historian L. D. Stillwell notes that Vermont experienced a population decrease of 10,000 to 15,000 between 1816 and 1817, reversing seven years of growth. Among those who left Vermont was the family of Joseph Smith, who relocated to Palmyra, New York. This move set off events that eventually led to Smith founding the Church of Jesus Christ of Latter-day Saints.

The incessant rain and gloomy weather in June 1816 confined Mary Shelley, Percy Bysshe Shelley, Lord Byron, John William Polidori, and their companions indoors at Villa Diodati during their Swiss holiday. Inspired by German ghost stories they had read, Lord Byron suggested a contest to write the scariest tale. This challenge led Mary Shelley to conceive "Frankenstein" and Byron to write "A Fragment," which Polidori later expanded into "The Vampyre," a precursor to "Dracula." These days indoors, marked by opium use and intellectual discourse, profoundly influenced Mary Shelley. One night, after an intense discussion, she envisioned Victor Frankenstein creating his monster, inspiring her novel. Lord Byron's poem "Darkness," inspired by a day so dim that "the fowls all went to roost at noon and candles had to be lit as at midnight," echoes the bleak conditions of the Year Without a Summer:

"I had a dream, which was not all a dream.
The bright sun was extinguish'd, and the stars
Did wander darkling in the eternal space,
Rayless, and pathless, and the icy earth
Swung blind and blackening in the moonless air;
Morn came and went—and came, and brought no day."

Justus von Liebig, a chemist who experienced the famine as a child in Darmstadt, later studied plant nutrition and pioneered the use of mineral fertilizers. His work was indirectly influenced by the agricultural struggles of this period, which underscored the importance of understanding and improving soil fertility to prevent future famines.

Chapter 4

Reflection questions

How did the eruption of Mount Tambora in 1815 contribute to global climate changes, and what were the immediate and long-term effects on different regions?

In what ways did the "Year Without a Summer" impact agricultural practices and food security in Europe and North America?

How did the climate anomalies of 1816 affect the socio-economic conditions in different parts of the world?

What role did the persistent "dry fog" and tephra in the atmosphere play in altering the visual art and literature of the early 19th century?

How did the scarcity of oats and other crops lead to technological innovations such as the invention of the draisine by Karl Drais?

In what ways did the climate crisis of 1816 influence migration patterns and settlement in the United States, particularly in New England and the Midwest?

How did the "Year Without a Summer" contribute to the rise of social and political movements, such as the abolitionist movement in upstate New York?

How did the adverse weather conditions of 1816 inspire literary works like Mary Shelley's "Frankenstein" and Lord Byron's poem "Darkness"?

What similarities can be drawn between the environmental impacts of the Tambora eruption and those of other notable volcanic eruptions, such as Krakatoa in 1883 and Mount Pinatubo in 1991?

How did the climate anomalies of the "Year Without a Summer" affect the daily lives and personal accounts of individuals, such as Sarah Snell Bryant and Thomas Jefferson?

What lessons can be learned from the response of communities to the climate crisis of 1816 in terms of resilience and adaptation?

How did the "Year Without a Summer" influence scientific advancements, particularly in the field of agriculture, as seen in the work of Justus von Liebig?

How did the visual representation of sunsets and atmospheric conditions in art from this period reflect the changes caused by the Tambora eruption?

In what ways did the climate anomalies of 1816 exacerbate existing social and economic inequalities, and how did different communities cope with these challenges?

How did the unusual weather patterns of 1816 affect global trade and economic systems, particularly in regions dependent on agriculture?

What role did environmental changes play in shaping historical events and cultural movements during the early 19th century?

How did the "Year Without a Summer" highlight the interconnectedness of natural events and human societies?

____

____

____

____

What insights can be gained from studying the "Year Without a Summer" in the context of contemporary climate change and environmental challenges?

____

____

____

____

How did the experiences of the "Year Without a Summer" influence the development of environmental science and meteorology?

What personal reflections or emotions did the history of the "Year Without a Summer" evoke in you as a reader, and how does this historical event resonate with modern-day climate concerns?

Chapter 5

Lessons learned

Global Interconnectedness: Natural events like volcanic eruptions can have worldwide effects, demonstrating the interconnectedness of our planet's systems.

Resilience and Adaptation: Communities must develop resilience and adapt to unforeseen climate challenges to ensure survival and stability.

Importance of Agricultural Diversity: Relying on a single crop can be risky; agricultural diversity can provide a buffer against climate anomalies.

Technological Innovation: Crises can drive technological advancements, as seen with Karl Drais's invention of the draisine due to the lack of oats.

Migration as an Adaptation Strategy: People historically moved to more hospitable regions in response to climate crises, a practice that continues today.

Economic Vulnerability: Disasters can expose economic vulnerabilities, especially in regions dependent on agriculture.

Social Unrest: Food shortages and economic hardships can lead to social unrest, emphasizing the need for effective crisis management and social safety nets.

Scientific Advancements: Environmental challenges can spur scientific research and innovations, as seen in advancements in agriculture and plant nutrition.

Art and Culture Reflect Environmental Changes: Artists and writers often reflect contemporary environmental conditions in their work, providing historical insights.

Impact on Public Health: Climate anomalies can exacerbate public health crises, as seen with the typhus epidemics in Europe.

Importance of Preparedness: Historical events highlight the need for preparedness and planning to mitigate the impacts of natural disasters.

Historical Perspective on Climate Change: Understanding past climate events can provide valuable insights into current and future climate change scenarios.

Role of Government and Institutions: Effective governance and institutional support are crucial in managing the impacts of natural disasters.

Cultural and Social Impacts: Climate events can significantly influence cultural and social dynamics, as seen with the migration and literary contributions of the period.

Environmental Awareness: Awareness of how natural events can impact the environment and human societies can foster better stewardship of the planet.

Long-term Consequences: The long-term effects of natural disasters can shape societal development, migration patterns, and economic structures.

Role of Communication: Effective communication of risks and conditions is vital in managing crises and supporting affected populations.

Historical Records as Learning Tools: Diaries, letters, and other historical records provide valuable lessons and insights into past events and responses.

Climate as a Driver of Change: Climate anomalies can drive significant social, economic, and technological changes.

Unity and Cooperation: Collective action and cooperation among communities, regions, and nations are essential in addressing and overcoming global challenges.

Conclusion

As we reach the conclusion of our journey through the fascinating history of the Year Without a Summer, it's essential to take a moment to reflect on the many aspects we've explored and to express my deepest gratitude to you, the reader, for investing your valuable time and resources into this biography. Without your engagement, this book would merely be words on a page; your curiosity and dedication bring it to life.

The eruption of Mount Tambora in April 1815 set off a chain of events that altered the course of history. From the high levels of tephra that painted the skies with rich red hues to the persistent "dry fog" that hung over the eastern United States, the volcanic winter reshaped the world in ways both subtle and profound. We've delved into the science behind these climatic changes and the art and literature that reflected this new reality. Paintings by artists like J. M. W. Turner and Caspar David Friedrich depicted the strikingly moody, darker scenes, a testament to the altered atmosphere.

The Year Without a Summer was not just a meteorological anomaly; it was a period of great human struggle and innovation. We explored how the severe crop failures led to widespread food shortages and social unrest, particularly in Europe and North America. Yet, from these hardships emerged remarkable resilience and ingenuity. The invention of the draisine by Karl Drais, driven by a scarcity of oats, is a prime example of how adversity can spur technological advancements.

Migration patterns were profoundly influenced by this climate crisis. Many left New England for the more hospitable Midwest, shaping the settlement patterns of the United States. This migration also played a role in centering the abolitionist movement in upstate New York, highlighting how environmental changes can drive social and political movements.

The cultural impact of the Year Without a Summer cannot be overstated. The dire conditions inspired literary giants like Mary Shelley and Lord Byron to create enduring works such as "Frankenstein" and "Darkness." These stories, born from the imagination stoked by an ungenial summer, continue to resonate with readers today.

Public health and economic structures were equally affected. The typhus epidemics and the dramatic rise in food prices underscored the vulnerabilities of societies dependent on stable agricultural conditions. The long-term consequences of such events remind us of the importance of preparedness and resilience in the face of natural disasters.

This historical exploration also brought to light the importance of scientific advancements. The work of Justus von Liebig, inspired by the famine he experienced as a child, led to significant progress in the field of plant nutrition. These advancements underscore how crises can catalyze scientific and technological progress that benefits future generations.

Dear reader, your engagement with this book is invaluable. Your curiosity, your willingness to delve into the past, and your passion for learning make this work meaningful. Without you, these stories, lessons, and reflections would remain untold. You breathe life into history by connecting with these narratives and drawing parallels to our present and future.

As we conclude, I humbly ask for your support. If you found this biography enlightening, engaging, or thought-provoking, please consider leaving a positive review. Your feedback not only helps other readers discover this book but also encourages the ongoing exploration and sharing of historical narratives. Your review is a powerful tool in ensuring that the lessons and stories of the Year Without a Summer continue to reach and inspire others.

Thank you once again for your time, your interest, and your support. It has been an honor to share this journey with you, and I hope that the insights gained will stay with you long after you turn the final page. Together, we keep the spirit of history alive and ensure that the stories of the past continue to inform and enrich our future.

www.ingramcontent.com/pod-product-compliance
Lightning Source LLC
Chambersburg PA
CBHW051708250726
48653CB00007B/2912